Titles in the series:

The Duck 0-241-11466-7
The Fox 0-241-11215-X
The Hedgehog 0-241-11467-5
The Mouse 0-241-11213-3
The Owl 0-241-11468-3
The Pigeon 0-241-11214-1
The Squirrel 0-241-11216-8
The Starling 0-241-11469-1

Design by Linda Rogers Associates

First Published in Great Britain 1985 by
Hamish Hamilton Children's Books
Garden House, 57 – 59 Long Acre, London WC2E 9JZ

British Library Cataloguing in Publication Data
Pope, Joyce
The owl.—(Animals in towns)
1. Owls—Juvenile literature
2. Urban fauna—Juvenile literature
I. Title II. Goss, Elizabeth III. Series
598'.97'091732 QL696.S8
ISBN 0-241-11468-3

Printed in Great Britain by
Blantyre Printing and Binding Ltd
London and Glasgow

Animals in Towns

The Owl

Joyce Pope

Illustrated by Elizabeth Goss

Hamish Hamilton · London

At night the people who lived near the town park often had trouble with their television sets. The picture would wobble and break up, but when the engineer came to mend the fault, he could never find anything wrong. It was all very mysterious.

The mystery would have been solved, though, if the people had gone outside to look at their aerials. Then they would have seen one of the most mysterious of the town's inhabitants, sitting and watching and listening – the tawny owl. The owl was well named, for her feathers were a dusky brown. Yet few people saw them as she slept for most of the day, and only came out to hunt in the evening. She wasn't interested in the television programmes she disrupted – they would have meant nothing to her. But she used the aerials as vantage points, from which to detect the slightest sound or movement that could mean a meal.

In the town, the bright street lights, shop windows and car headlamps enabled the owl to see quite clearly. But even on dark, moonless nights, she hunted successfully. Like a cat, her huge eyes could open wide to take in every scrap of light.

The owl also used her ears to hunt, and would often hear the rustle made by a mouse or vole as it scurried through the undergrowth. Her ears weren't as noticeable as her eyes, lying one on each side of her head beneath feathers which were looser and finer than anywhere else on her body. The ears themselves were partly covered by flaps of skin. These she could move to funnel any tiny sound and so hear it better.

And like a cat she could move silently. All her feathers, even those on her wings, were so soft that she made no noise at all as she drifted down on to her prey.

Although the owl was so soft, a sharp beak lay almost hidden in the feathers of her face, and her toes were armed with talons so powerful they could kill a mouse in a flash. When she hunted, she flew towards her prey and, at the last moment, swung her legs forward, to seize it between her claws.

She caught different food at different times of the year. In the summer, she fed well on mice and sparrows, and foolish young blackbirds she snatched from their roosts. Sometimes she caught beetles, or marched across the football pitch grabbing fat earthworms which had left their burrows in search of leaves to feed on. In the winter, she fed mostly on small birds, raiding the big roosts of starlings and sometimes even catching a pigeon weakened by the cold.

The owl wasted very little time eating the food she caught. Her beak opened wide enough for her to swallow most things in one great big gulp. Only when she was lucky and caught a big rat or pigeon, did she have to tear it up with her sharp bill.

When she had fed, the owl retreated to one of her safe resting places. Here she usually dozed for a while, and then woke up, looking a bit uncomfortable. A few moments later she would spit out a sausage-shaped pellet made of all the bones and feathers or fur of the animal she had swallowed a short time ago. In this way, she got rid of anything she could not digest, even tiny things like the hard legs or wing cases of beetles, or the minute hairs that earthworms wear along their bodies. In time quite a pile of pellets built up below her roosting place. Anyone looking at them would have been able to tell what she had been feeding on.

During the day, the owl rested. She usually sat half covered by the leaves of a great ivy plant that wound its way into the branches of an old oak tree. Her brown feathers made her difficult to see in the shade. One day, a boy who was looking for a lost ball glanced up and saw her. He wasn't sure whether or not he could really see a bird, so he walked round the tree to try and get a better view. The owl knew that he was there and as he walked she kept an eye on him. Even when he was behind her she could still see him, because she was able to turn her head right round and look over her back.

Although she normally disliked bright light, in the early summer the owl would sometimes sunbathe. She would sit on the ground facing the sun with her head thrown back and her eyes closed. She spread her wings wide and opened her beak, as though drinking in the warmth. But she never stayed like this for very long, because a sharp-eyed wren or starling would see her and scream a warning to all the other birds nearby. The owl would fly quietly back to her usual roost.

Sometimes, when the wind changed and ruffled her feathers, the owl would look for a new place to rest. When she did this, she usually had trouble from the small birds, none of which liked to have an owl about.

A great tit, searching for spiders or insects on the trunk of the tree, was usually the first to see her. Keeping a good way off, because it was frightened of the owl's talons and beak, it would start to jerk its tail and wings and give a screaming call. Soon it would be joined by other birds – sparrows and starlings, robins and wrens – as well as many others, all twittering and screeching.

Sometimes, their noise would be too much for the owl and she would give up and go back to her usual spot. At other times, she would just close her eyes and ignore the fuss, and eventually the little birds would go away. But they would avoid that tree for a long time afterwards, in case the owl was still there.

Although she lived and hunted alone, the owl knew there were other owls about, for she often heard one calling in the distance when she was out looking for food. One evening in early spring, the hooting seemed nearer than usual. The owl answered with a cry that sounded like 'kee-wick'. Over

the next few nights, the two owls sang their wavering whistles and cries to each other, until one moonlight evening, the owl saw the newcomer for the first time. He was sitting quietly on a tree near the edge of her hunting ground.

The owl flew down close to him, snapping her bill angrily. But although he was smaller than she was, the male owl did not fly away. Instead he stepped back along the branch, sleeking his feathers to his body. Then, almost before she could do anything he moved towards her again, puffing his feathers out, and raising one wing. Then he backed away again, bobbing and swaying and grunting as he did so.

For some time the owl moved very little, but then she began to sway with the movement of the male. Every night he courted her in this way, and each time she joined more actively in the dance, until one night they mated. After this, they often sat close together, nibbling and preening each other's feathers, and making small chuckling noises which nobody else could hear. They flew round the town and park together, looking for somewhere to make a nest. The best sort of place would have been a deep hole in a hollow tree, but the park was very tidy and didn't have any dead trees. They even looked at a wide ledge on the face of the town hall, but that was too exposed.

Eventually they decided on a rather small hole in an old tree in an overgrown garden. Here, in the middle of March, the owl laid her first egg. It was white and almost round, and as soon as it was laid she settled down to keep it warm. Two days later she laid her second egg and two days after this, a third to complete the clutch.

For exactly a month the owl brooded her eggs, while her mate worked hard to collect enough food for them both. Then the first of the chicks hatched. It was covered with thick down, which almost hid its sharp beak, and had big, alert, pink-rimmed eyes. The owl still kept the other eggs warm, for they were not yet ready to hatch. But two days later, the second chick broke from its shell and two days after that the third one emerged. The family was complete.